25 Folksong Solos for Children

Easy Arrangements for Voice and Piano
Especially Created for Young Singers

To access companion recorded accompaniments online, visit:
www.halleonard.com/mylibrary

Enter Code
7605-2762-1722-8428

ISBN 978-1-4950-5411-2

7777 W. BLUEMOUND RD. P.O. BOX 13819 MILWAUKEE, WI 53213

In Australia Contact:
Hal Leonard Australia Pty. Ltd.
4 Lentara Court
Cheltenham, Victoria, 3192 Australia
Email: ausadmin@halleonard.com.au

Visit Hal Leonard Online at
www.halleonard.com

Stream or download piano accompaniment recordings
by using the access code on the title page at:
www.halleonard.com/mylibrary

25 Folksong Solos for Children

Contents

Pianists on the recordings: [1] Brendan Fox, [2] Joshua Parman, [3] Richard Walters, [4] Laura Ward

ANIMAL FAIR

American Folksong
Arranged by Joel K. Boyd

This page has been left blank to facilitate page turns.

ALL THE PRETTY LITTLE HORSES

Southeastern American Lullaby
Arranged by Brendan Fox

Slowly rocking, delicately ♩ = 68

Hush-you-bye, don't you cry, go to sleep-y lit-tle ba - by. When you wake, you shall have all the pret-ty lit-tle hors - es.

A little faster

Blacks and bays, dap-ples and greys, coach and six-a-lit-tle hors - es.

Tempo I

Blacks and bays, dap-ples and greys, coach and six-a-lit-tle hors - es. Hush-you-bye,

ANNABEL LEE

American Folksong
Arranged by Brendan Fox

THE ASH GROVE

Welsh Folksong
Arranged by Joshua Parman

BILL GROGAN'S GOAT

Southern Appalachian Folksong
Arranged by Brendan Fox

CRADLE SONG
(Kehto Laulu)

Finnish Folksong
Arranged by Joshua Parman

Lyrics: Ding dong, back and forth it goes; The cra-dle rocks the child to sleep so soon. Ding dong, while the cra-dle swings, moth-er has a lull-a-by to croon.

Ding dong, how the fid - dle plays, And hap - py chil - dren dance now to the tune. Ding dong, out the door you go; Live your life, for it is o - ver soon.

EVERY NIGHT WHEN THE SUN GOES IN

Southern Appalachian
Arranged by Brendan Fox

FATHER'S WHISKERS

American Folksong
Arranged by Joshua Parman

now it's all caved in. He stepped up-on his whisk-ers and_ walked up to his chin. When

Fa-ther goes in swim-ming, no bath-ing suit for him. He ties his whisk-ers 'round his waist and

then he plung-es in. They're al-ways in the way, the cows eat them for hay. They

hide the dirt on dad-dy's shirt they're al-ways in the way.

THE GENEROUS FIDDLER

German Folksong
Arranged by Benjamin M. Culli

waiting with impatient feet. Fiddler,
poor and humble folk are we." "Naught care

fiddler, come you soon, and play us all a
I for what you say! If you must dance then

merry tune.
I must play." Tra la - la-la-la-la-la, Tra la-la-la-

la-la, Tra la - la-la-la-la-la, Tra la - la - la.

HOW CAN I KEEP FROM SINGING

Words possibly by
Anna Bartlett Warner

Music possibly by
Robert Wadsworth Lowry
Adapted by Brendan Fox
from an arrangement by Christopher Ruck

When ty - rants trem - ble, sick with fear And hear their death knells ring - ing; When friends re - joice both far and near, How can I keep from sing - ing? In pris - on cell and dun - geon vile Our thoughts to them are wing - ing. When friends by shame are __

LITTLE BROWN DOG

American Folksong
Arranged by Joshua Parman

round the world in half a day, and on him I could ride.
all the walls of Lon - don came a tum - bling to the ground.

Sing fad - dle - o day. _____ I

I bought _ me a

lit - tle hen, all speck - led and fair. I sat her on an oy - ster shell; she

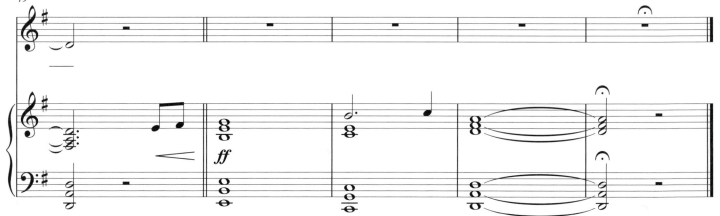

HUSH, LITTLE BABY

Carolina Folk Lullaby
Arranged by Richard Walters

Gently, a lullaby ♩ = c. 69

Hush, lit-tle ba-by, don't say a word, Pa-pa's gon-na buy you a mock-in'-bird.

If that mock-in'-bird don't sing, Pa-pa's gon-na buy you a dia-mond ring.____

If that dia-mond

THE LARK IN THE MORN

Irish Folksong
Arranged by Brendan Fox

MY WHITE HORSE
(Mi caballo blanco)

Chilean Folksong
Arranged by Joshua Parman

THE WATER IS WIDE

Traditional
Arranged by Brendan Fox

ON MONDAYS I NEVER GO TO WORK

Traditional
Arranged by Brendan Fox

Light and bouncy ♩ = 90

On Mon - days I nev - er go to work. On Tues - days I stay at home. On Wednes - days I

nev - er feel in - clined. Work is the last thing on my mind. On Thurs - days it's a

THE MERMAID

18th Century Sea Chantey
Arranged by Brendan Fox

'Twas Fri - day __ morn when we __ set __ sail, And we were not far from the land, When our cap - tain __ spied a love - ly mer - maid With a comb and a glass in her hand. Oh, the o - cean waves may roll, And the

POOR LONESOME COWBOY

Traditional
Arranged by Richard Walters

I __ ain't got no moth - er, I __ ain't got no moth - er, I __

ain't got no moth - er to mend the clothes I wear. I'm a poor lone - some

cow - boy, I'm a poor lone - some cow - boy, I'm a poor lone - some cow - boy and a

long way from home. I __ ain't got no sis - ter, I __

THE RED RIVER VALLEY

Traditional American Cowboy Song
Arranged by Benjamin M. Culli

sun - shine _____ that has bright - ened our path - way a -
break - in' _____ and the grief that you are caus - in'

while.
me.

Come and sit by my side if you love me. _____ Do not

has - ten to bid me ad - ieu. Just re - mem - ber the Red Riv - er

Val - ley, _____ and the {girl}{boy} that has loved you so true.

SCARBOROUGH FAIR

English Folksong
Adapted by Brendan Fox
from an arrangement by Christopher Ruck

poco rit.

was
know { he's / she's } a true love of mine.

poco rit.

mf

mine.

p freely

a tempo

I must know { he's / she's } a true love of mine.

colla voce

a tempo

rit.

rit.

SIMPLE GIFTS

Traditional Shaker Song
Arranged by Richard Walters

THE STREETS OF LAREDO

American Cowboy Song
Arranged by Richard Walters

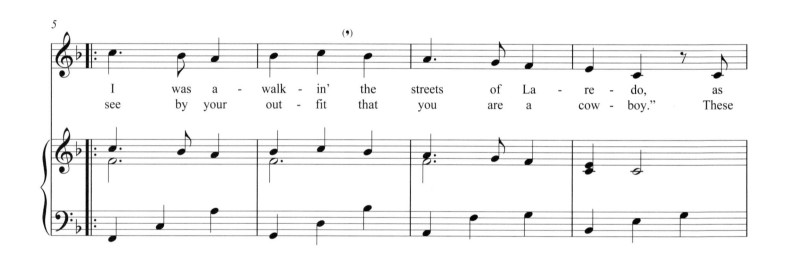

I was a-walk-in' the streets of La-re-do, as
see by your out-fit that you are a cow-boy." These

I walked out in La-re-do one day I spied a young
words he said as I bold-ly walked by. "Come sit down be-

cow - boy all wrapped in white lin - en, all wrapped in white
side me and hear my sad sto - ry, I'm shot in the

lin - en and cold as the clay.
chest and I know I must

"I die."

"Oh bang the drum slow - ly and play the fife

SHENANDOAH

19th Century American Chanty
Arranged by Benjamin M. Culli

SWEET THE EVENING AIR OF MAY

English Folksong
Arranged by Richard Walters

Andante, Sweetly ♩ = c. 72

Sweet, the eve-ning air of May, soft my cheek ca-ress - ing.

Sweet, the un-seen li-lacs spray with its scent-ed bless - ing.

White and ghost-ly in the gloom shine the ap-ple trees in bloom,

TELL ME WHY

American Folksong
Arranged by Benjamin M. Culli

Smoothly, with an easy flow